S0-AJY-048

6 Reasons
for
Faith

Mark Weimer

LCX

LIFE CONNEXIONS
PEACHTREE CITY, GA

6 Reasons for Faith

Published by Life ConneXions
The Publishing Group of Campus Crusade for Christ
375 Highway 74 South, Suite A
Peachtree City, GA 30269
To order: (800) 827-2788

© 2006 Campus Crusade for Christ, Inc. All rights reserved.
No part of this book may be reproduced, stored in a retrieval
system, or transmitted in any form or by any means, except
in the case of brief quotations printed in articles or reviews,
without prior permission in writing from the publisher.

All Scripture quotations, unless otherwise indicated, are taken
from the Holy Bible: New International Version, © 1973,
1978, 1984 by the International Bible Society. Published by
Zondervan Bible Publishers, Grand Rapids, Michigan.

Printed in the United States of America

ISBN: 1-56399-275-2

Table of Contents

Introduction

The purpose of this book is to get you to think.

Can I prove to you beyond a doubt that God exists? I can't — all I can do is to give you reasons to consider faith in God.

I just had lunch with a friend who said he thought there was virtually no evidence for the existence of God. I told him I thought he was wrong — that, if you looked, you could find many reasons to believe in God.

Billions of people in the world believe in God. If they are right, then the most important decision you will ever make in life is whether to believe. This book can not make you choose to believe — only you can do that. But I hope this book may bring some light to help you consider the existence of God.

So I encourage you to read this short book with an open mind — and be open to God.

REASON 1

The Wonder Of Nature

Imagine walking through the desert on a hot afternoon. Suddenly you see a metallic glint in the distance and race over to investigate. You find a fine watch that looks like it has been buried in the sand for many years. You pick it up and examine it; the watch is still running. You put it on your wrist. The watch works beautifully and tells perfect time.

Would you say to yourself "Isn't it amazing that this watch just created itself from nothing here in the desert after all these years?" Of course not. You would instantly understand that anything as complex as a watch must surely have an expert watchmaker that made it.

Now take a look at the world around you. As I am writing this I look out my back window and see beautiful trees; a sunlit sky; and colorful vines in gorgeous fall colors. The world is infinitely more complex than a watch. Would I just say, "Isn't it amazing how these things have all just formed themselves here in such beauty and how they work so well all by themselves?" Or would I say, "Who created all this beauty?" Isn't it possible that, as the Bible says, "In the beginning God created the heavens and the earth?"[1]

Now picture, if you can, a DNA molecule. DNA is the genetic "instruction book" which gives guidance to our cells within our body. The Nobel Prize was won by scientists who investigated the highly complex "double helix" of DNA. DNA is the "building block" of life. In a DNA molecule, elaborate systems all work together to give detailed instructions to each cell. 2,000 instructions per second — over 100 million instructions per day — are given so that each cell knows exactly what to do. DNA molecules can store more information than the most sophisticated computer today. A single gram of DNA can hold as much information as a trillion (1,000,000,000,000) CD's. In fact, one pound of DNA could contain more computer memory than all the electronic computers ever made.

Could something as sophisticated as this have simply happened by chance? It certainly is possible mathematically. However, if you traveled to a foreign planet and came across something which had the sophistication of a modern computer, you would probably conclude that it had been built by someone.

The beauty of creation is a silent testimony to a master artist who created all things. In speaking about God, Isaiah the prophet said "He who created the heavens, He is God; He who fashioned and made the earth, He founded it; He did not create it to be empty…"[2] Isn't it interesting that, even in this modern day and age, a majority of people on this earth believe that the world was created by God?

Nature itself can be very beautiful. Some of the most beautiful paintings done by man are simply of nature scenes. For a project, you could take a walk outside some morning. Look at the beauty of the sunrise and the colors that are splashed across the sky. King David said, "The heavens declare the glory of God; the skies proclaim the work of His hands."[3] Take a walk in a garden, if you have one near you, and look at the beauty of a flower. Think of the intricate way that nature is woven together, as trees and flowers sprout anew each year.

Charles Darwin put forth, in the 1850's, the proposition that everything we see on earth happened by random chance as a result of natural selection. Is it possible that this happened? Certainly it is possible; a large number of things are possible.

Now let's look at the odds that everything we see actually did happen by random chance. Let's take just the likelihood that the earliest and simplest living cell could have formed spontaneously. It has been estimated that the odds against this are greater than the odds that you could find a single specific grain of sand in the Sahara Desert while blindfolded — odds greater than 100,000,000,000,000 to one.

If you were asked to bet a significant sum of money on something with odds against it of 100,000,000,000,000 to one, you would be foolish to wager more than a penny. Yet that is exactly what we are doing when we assume that the combination of elements necessary for life, the universe and all that it contains simply evolved by random chance. Is it possible that it happened by random chance? Certainly. Is it likely? I wouldn't bet a significant amount of money against odds like that.

Think about the beauty of nature and the complexity of this world. A great scientist can spend his whole life investigating just one little portion of the world. When we observe the beautiful complexity of creation, should we not say "How great is God — beyond our understanding!"[4] Some of the greatest minds on earth have spent 30 or 40 years investigating a tiny particle of creation. For example, one noted British scientist spent 30 years just categorizing thousands of types of one little plant, the fern.

DNA findings now also shed an interesting light on our common ancestry. It is now believed with modern DNA testing we may be able to trace all living human beings back to a single set of common ancestors in the not too distant past. What does the Bible say? "So God created man in His own image, in the image of God He created him; male and female He created them."[5]

Let's take a quick look at the "big bang theory." In the early 1900's, there were two major contradictory theories about how the entire universe began. One theory, according to Christianity and other religions, said that God created the universe from nothing at a single point in time. The other theory, held largely by those who did not believe in the existence of God, was that the universe had always existed and had no creator.

So what has science discovered in the last 30 years? Science has discovered that the entire universe is rapidly expanding and that, as far as we can tell, it all began at a single point. In other words, the universe has not always existed; it came into being at a single point in time. The next obvious questions are "What happened before that point? What caused this big bang to occur?" When an astronomy professor at Stanford University was asked this question, he smiled and said "You are in the wrong department." He said we would have to leave the department of science and go to another department — such as philosophy or religion — to answer this question.

That professor was a wise man to recognize the limits of his knowledge. The Bible says in the book of Romans "For since the creation of the world God's invisible qualities — His eternal power and divine nature — have been clearly seen, being understood from what has been made, so that men are without excuse."[6]

So consider these thoughts:

1. The odds of all nature having been created by random chance are billions to 1. You have two choices: either someone created all of this, or

there is an extremely small chance that it was created randomly. Which do you choose?

2. Recent scientific discoveries make it likely that the universe was created at a single point in time in a "big bang." The Bible says, "God created the heavens and the earth."[7] Throughout human history, most people have believed that God created the heavens and the earth. Modern science now agrees that our entire universe was created at a single point in time.

3. Consider the beauty of life — flowers, animals, the beautiful sky — could this have happened randomly? If you went to a museum and saw a beautiful painting, would you say "How amazing that the paints just fell this way by random chance?" Or would you be more likely to say "What wonderful artist created this beautiful painting?"

Is it likely that everything just happened to turn out so beautifully and that it all works together so well? Or is it more likely that all of these scientific virtual impossibilities lead us to one simple answer — that God created the heavens and the earth and all mankind? The simple explanation is that the Bible

is correct — God created everything. If you choose
to believe there is no God, the odds are against you.
It's your choice.

REASON 2

What About
Good And Evil?

Was Adolf Hitler a bad person? The answer to this seems obvious. "Of course he was," almost everyone today would say. But to a majority of Germans in the 1930's, Hitler was a good man and many Germans supported his policies. If morality is just a matter of public opinion, was Hitler really good in the 1930's? Or maybe Hitler was good to Germans but bad to everyone else. Does anyone even have the right to call him bad? Don't you know in your heart that Hitler was bad, even if 1930's Germany voted for him?

What makes something or someone good or evil? In the Bible, when Adam and Eve ate from the tree, they were given the knowledge of good and evil. Christians believe that since that time mankind as a whole has had an innate sense of good and evil, and of right and wrong.

Then again, perhaps good and evil are just a matter of popular vote; whatever the majority of people decide makes something either right or wrong. In fact, many countries would take this position. In the United States, polls are continually taken to determine whether a majority of people feel that, for example, a practice like abortion is wrong.

However, if good and evil are just determined by a majority vote, then what do we make of situations like slavery in the United States? From the founding of America in 1776 until the Civil War in 1863, slavery was determined to be legal. A majority of Americans and a majority of states allowed for the holding of slaves for much of that time. But did this make slavery right? Today, almost all people would agree that slavery is wrong. Jesus taught us to "Do to others as you would have them do to you."[1] If we followed this rule, then obviously we would determine that slavery is wrong, because none of us would want to be enslaved.

The Bible paints a clear contrast to the view that morality comes from popular vote; it states that morality and good and evil are determined by God.

For all eternity, to "love your neighbor as yourself"[2] has been good. In the same way, other acts, like stealing bread from a poor person, are evil.

Some might say that the government is who determines good and evil. For example, before the 1960's it was legal to pray in schools in the United States, but after a Supreme Court decision, it was no longer legal. Does this mean that prayer in schools was morally good in the 1950's and morally evil in the 1980's? Of course not. Government rulings do not change morality. Hopefully governments will make good rules, but they cannot always be counted on to determine what is good and moral.

Another example is communism. In Soviet Russia in the early 1900's, it was determined that the state — the government — was the ultimate determiner of good and evil. Stalin, the head of Russia, decided that millions of Russians should be killed because they represented the old regime. Was this good because it was determined by the government? If you take God out of the equation, then what right would you have to say that Stalin was wrong in killing millions of innocent people? If the state decides right and wrong, then was Stalin morally right since he represented the state?

Christians believe, and the Bible states, that God is the ultimate source of morality — of what is good and evil. The Bible says about God, "All Your words are true; all Your righteous laws are eternal."[3] God's character is good; as the Bible also says "God is love."[4] The very nature of God embodies all that is good, and this will never change.

Our own spiritual "gut feelings" also tell us of the existence of good and evil. The Bible says "The fruit of the Spirit is love, joy, peace, patience, kindness, goodness, faithfulness, gentleness and self-control."[5] Don't our hearts yearn for these things? Don't we all sense in our spirit that these qualities, which come from God, are somehow inherently good?

Let's contrast that with what the Bible says are qualities that can come from our hearts when we are away from God — "hatred, discord, jealousy, fits of rage, selfish ambition..."[6] Which would you rather have? A world filled with love, joy, peace, kindness and goodness — or a world filled with strife, war, jealousy and hatred? This is not a matter of putting it to a vote; our own innate sense tells us the difference between right and wrong. A world filled with peace and love and joy would be morally good, even if the majority of people voted for a world filled with hatred.

If we are looking for another explanation that doesn't involve God, then maybe good and evil are just determined by biology. Perhaps it is all a matter of our hormones and genes and chemical makeup. One problem with this is what if someone says they are just not biologically or chemically wired that way? A murderer might say "I just couldn't help myself. I didn't know what I did was wrong." What if the people who are running a country seem to have no biological sense of morality, as was the case with Pol Pot in Cambodia who killed millions of his countrymen in the 1970's? Could Pol Pot simply say "I'm sorry, I'm not wired that way?" In a recent interview he seemed genuinely puzzled that people would think what he did was wrong.

It is possible that someone may not think something is wrong, even if it is. The Bible says "There is a way that seems right to a man, but in the end it leads to death."[7] Sometimes appearances can be deceiving and we can confuse what is right with what is wrong. But even if our subjective judgment is confused, don't most of us know innately that some actions are right and some actions are wrong?

Think of some things that are good and others that are evil. What if your country determined that some good things are illegal and bad things are legal. How would that make you feel if your country said it was good to kill helpless people, and bad to care for the poor?

Mother Teresa was a Catholic nun who served most of her life in India. She started an order called the Sisters of Charity. Their mission was largely to care for the poor and dying in Calcutta, India. She gave of herself unselfishly. At one point, during a visit to San Francisco, she determined that the accommodations given to her were too luxurious and asked that the bed be replaced with a simpler bed so that she and her followers wouldn't get spoiled by luxury.

What made Mother Teresa good? If no one noticed or applauded her, would she still have carried out her actions? Whether anyone noticed or not, her actions were still good.

Without God, morality can be just a shifting sea of differing opinions. For example, almost all societies and religions have similar moral codes; it is good to be kind, but it is bad to steal, murder and lie. A common theme through almost all of these societies and religions would be that these are absolute values given by God. Take God out of the equation, say that all values are relative or determined by society, and the moral difference between Mother Teresa and Adolf Hitler is based on the latest public opinion poll. Regardless of what your mind or philosophy would tell you, don't you know in your heart that there truly is good and there truly is evil? The Bible teaches that good comes from God. God has given you the ability to know the difference between good and evil.

REASON 3

Our Empty Hearts

Marilyn Monroe was a beautiful actress in American movies in the 1950's. She seemingly had it all — good looks, fame, fortune and a string of famous husbands. She was the envy of millions of people and seemed to be on top of life. Yet in 1962 she took her own life, alone in a motel room.

In recent years, the New England Patriots of the National Football League won three Super Bowls. This is the height of achievement in American sports, and Tom Brady, the quarterback of the Patriots, was the man who led them to these championships. Tom seemingly has it all. He has achieved what few people in professional sports have ever done and he is young, single, famous and well paid. Yet he was recently quoted by CBSNews.com as saying "Why do I have three Super Bowl rings and still think there's something greater out there for me? I think, 'God, it's got to be more than this.'"

Most of us spend all of our lives searching for fame, money or the right job promotion which we believe will give us the happiness we've been seeking. Solomon was the king of Israel almost 3,000 years ago and had tremendous fame and fortune. The Bible says he possessed more wealth than any king who had existed before him. He had great riches, hundreds of wives, and peace in his kingdom.

Yet when Solomon surveyed all that he had accomplished and acquired, he said "What does man gain from all his labor at which he toils under the sun?"[1] Even though Solomon was a king who had it all in terms of riches, power, women and fame, he realized that "when I surveyed all that my hands had done and what I had toiled to achieve, everything was meaningless, a chasing after the wind; nothing was gained under the sun."[2] Apart from God, Solomon discovered there is no ultimate meaning in life.

Why is it that we spend so much of our lives striving for a promotion, enough money or some event which we think will make us happy, only to find that when we achieve it, it does not satisfy the longing of our soul? The Bible answers this by saying that only

God can truly satisfy our souls. The letter to Hebrew Christians says "Keep your lives free from the love of money and be content with what you have, because God has said, 'Never will I leave you; never will I forsake you.'" [3] It is God's presence that can bring true happiness.

In the 1960's one of the most famous rock and roll musicians in the United States was Jimi Hendrix. He was a legendary guitar player who was the closing act at the Woodstock music festival and played all over Europe and America. His guitar solos are still regarded as possibly the finest guitar playing of all time. Sex, drugs and rock and roll characterized his lifestyle. At the height of his popularity he died, full of drugs, in his own vomit. Earthly success did not bring him lasting happiness.

From the day we are born, we are often led to believe that it is by meeting our goals that we will acquire happiness. Picture a young girl named Ellen, in the first grade, taking her first big test. She gets an "A" and is happy for a day or two, only to find out there is another test the following week. Soon she starts worrying and striving for that next goal.

When Ellen goes out for sports, she joins the school soccer team. She then becomes convinced that if her team can just win the championship, it will be the greatest thing in the world. Next for Ellen comes college, then getting her first car, then getting the right job, then finding the right husband, then having children, then having her children succeed, then meeting her family's financial needs. Now Ellen is at the end of her life, and what does it all mean?

One of the greatest arguments for the existence of God is the fact that nothing can truly satisfy the human spirit apart from God. The famed French scientist Pascal said "There is a God-shaped vacuum in the heart of every man which cannot be filled by any created thing, but only by God the Creator, made known through Jesus Christ." Jesus said, "Peace I leave with you; My peace I give you. I do not give to you as the world gives. Do not let your hearts be troubled and do not be afraid."[4] Maybe you've spent your life chasing after a goal that you've never achieved, or maybe you've achieved a goal only to find that it didn't bring the lasting satisfaction you thought it would.

A businessman named Bill, who I worked with years ago, described how it felt when he bought a new Porsche sports car. He said that the first night he owned it he went out into the garage and looked at it and thought about how great the car was. The second day he looked at it again, but it didn't look quite as great as the first night. By the end of the first week, while he still enjoyed having the car, it no longer brought him the thrill and satisfaction that he had when he first bought the car.

I once took a philosophy class at Stanford University. The professor was an excellent teacher and described, with great enthusiasm, many of the great philosophical approaches to life. Each one was different and gave a different point of view. I remember someone asking the professor which he personally believed, and I remember him saying, in spite of his great learning, that he did not know.

All of the education in the world cannot give you lasting peace in your heart. The Bible tells us "Do not be anxious about anything, but in everything, by prayer and petition, with thanksgiving, present your requests to God. And the peace of God, which transcends all understanding, will guard your hearts and your minds in Christ Jesus."[5] God's peace in our hearts is greater than all human understanding.

In the first century, Christians were often persecuted by the Roman government. History records how Christian martyrs were led into the Coliseum to be torn to pieces by wild beasts. As they entered the Coliseum, they would often sing praises to God. How can this be? If happiness comes from money, circumstance or security, then these Christians should have been the most miserable people in the world. In earthly terms, they had lost it all and were about to meet a horrible fate. Yet, they were filled with joy because they saw an eternity in heaven beyond their circumstances.

You can have God's peace and joy in your heart when you ask Jesus Christ to be your savior. David, in praying to God in the Bible, said "You will fill me with joy in Your presence."[6] Without Christ in your life, you could make millions of dollars and achieve every goal you have and still come to the end of your life empty.

God designed us to have a relationship with Him. Back in the Garden of Eden, God would spend time with Adam and Eve and talk to them as friends would talk to each other. Man was created to have a relationship with God, but we often spend our time chasing illusions that we think will bring us happiness.

Did your last promotion really give you lasting happiness? Did the last thing you bought really give you lasting satisfaction in your heart? Achieving earthly goals can bring temporary satisfaction, but ultimate peace only comes from having Christ in your life.

REASON 4

Who Is Jesus?

B ill Bright, the founder of Campus Crusade for Christ, tells of meeting with a college student and asking him who, in his opinion, was the greatest leader the world had ever known. The student thought and, even though he was a follower of an Eastern religion, said it was Jesus. Bill asked who was the greatest teacher; the student said "The greatest teacher is Jesus." Then Bill asked who in history had lived the most holy life. The student answered "There has never been anyone like Jesus."

For almost 2,000 years, men and women from different countries and religions have stood in awe of Jesus Christ. Even those who are not Christians recognize that Jesus lived an amazing life on this earth.

In coming to this earth, Jesus fulfilled dozens of prophecies. Jesus was His given name; the word

Christ refers to His being the Messiah, the Savior. It was prophesied that the Messiah would be born of a virgin, and born in Bethlehem. Jesus fulfilled these prophecies: the virgin Mary was His mother and He was born in Bethlehem, the ancestral home of King David.

King Herod inquired of the Jewish leaders "where the Christ was to be born. 'In Bethlehem in Judea,' they replied, 'for this is what the prophet has written: "But you, Bethlehem, in the land of Judah, are by no means least among the rulers of Judah; for out of you will come a ruler who will be the shepherd of my people Israel."'" [1] Jesus fulfilled dozens of other prophecies in the Old Testament in His life, death and resurrection.

As described in the Bible, Christ worked many miracles while here on earth. He said that God was His Father, and that He could only do the things that He saw His Father do. At one time a man who was lame was brought to Jesus. This man could not walk, but his friends lowered him on a bed in front of Jesus. Jesus said to him, "Son, your sins are forgiven."[2] Seeing the reaction of religious leaders around Him who said "Who can forgive sins but God alone?"[3] Jesus said, "'Which is easier: to say to the paralytic, "Your sins are forgiven," or to say, "Get up, take your mat and walk"? But that you may know that the Son of Man has authority on earth to forgive sins…' He said to the paralytic, 'I tell you, get up, take your mat and go home.' He got up, took his mat and walked out in full view of them all."[4]

On another occasion, a friend of Jesus' named Lazarus had died. Four days after Lazarus died, Jesus came to the town of Bethany and was met by Lazarus' sisters, Mary and Martha. Jesus said to Martha "'I am the resurrection and the life. He who believes in Me will live, even though he dies; and whoever lives and believes in Me will never die. Do you believe this?' 'Yes, Lord,' she told Him, 'I believe that You are the Christ, the Son of God, who was to come into the world.'"[5]

Jesus then came to the tomb where a gravestone covered the tomb. "'Take away the stone,' He said….'Did I not tell you that if you believed, you would see the glory of God?'"[6] Jesus then prayed and "called in a loud voice, 'Lazarus, come out!'"[7] and Lazarus, who had died four days before, walked alive out of the tomb.

On another occasion, Jesus fed 5,000 people when He miraculously multiplied just a few loaves of bread and a few fish. When the people came seeking Him afterwards, He told them not to seek Him because of the food; because far more important was eternal food. He said to them, "I am the bread of life…I am the living bread that came down from heaven. If anyone eats of this bread, he will live forever."[8]

Jesus came to earth not only to live and to teach us, but to die for our sins. Jesus willingly chose to go to Jerusalem even though He knew that He would be crucified there. The religious leaders turned Him over to the Romans to be crucified because He said He was the Messiah, the Son of God. When His followers resisted the soldiers, He told them to put away their swords, acknowledging that He was going willingly to His crucifixion. He said "Do you think I cannot call on My Father, and He will at once put at My disposal more than twelve legions of angels?"[9] Even while being crucified, Jesus prayed for those who were striking the nails into His hands and feet, saying "Father, forgive them, for they do not know what they are doing."[10]

Mel Gibson, in his movie "The Passion of the Christ," paints a gripping picture of the last 24 hours of Jesus' life, including the agony of His crucifixion. It is difficult for us to conceive of the horrors of a

Roman crucifixion, including being terribly beaten and then nailed to a cross to linger and die. On the day Christians honor as Good Friday, Jesus was crucified in the morning. The sky was dark from noon until three in the afternoon. At three, Jesus said "Father, into Your hands I commit My spirit,"[11] and gave up His life to God.

The best place to learn about Jesus' life is in the four Gospels contained in the New Testament of the Bible — Matthew, Mark, Luke and John. All of these books were written in the first century following Christ's death. Our understanding is that Matthew was written by the disciple Matthew, one of Jesus' twelve disciples. Mark was written by John Mark, who traveled with the apostle Peter and learned about Jesus' life from him. Luke was written by a non-Jewish doctor who traveled with the apostle Paul. John was written by the beloved apostle John, one of Jesus' twelve disciples. All four are based on eyewitness accounts of the life and death of Jesus Christ.

If what Jesus said about Himself is true — that He truly is the Son of God who died for your sins and mine — then learning about Jesus is the most important thing you can do. You can read the Gospel of Matthew, which has 28 chapters, and finish at a leisurely pace in a month by reading one chapter a day. As you read, you can ask God to help you to know Jesus in a personal way.

Back to our history — when Jesus died, one might have thought that the story of Jesus was over. Even His disciples were uncertain as to their future. But after three days, on the day we now celebrate as Easter Sunday, Jesus rose from the dead. When Mary Magdalene and another woman came to the tomb to anoint Jesus' body, they were met by two angels who said "Why do you look for the living among the dead? He is not here; He has risen!"[12]

As you read the accounts of Jesus' death and resurrection, which can be found near the end of each of the four gospels, think of how this could relate to you. For example, do you have sins in your life? Of course you do. None of us are perfect. All of us have thought or done things that are wrong. If you think you've done nothing wrong, then you're probably guilty of the sin of pride.

Whether lying, stealing, envying others or selfishly caring for ourselves and not for others, we've all committed sins. The meaning of Jesus' death was that He suffered punishment rather than us having to pay for our sins. We deserve punishment for our sins. He, who had committed no sin, did not deserve any punishment, but He took our punishment in our place.

The celebration of Easter paints a picture of the resurrection of Christ and the fact that He conquered death. Early Christians used to greet each other in this way: One would say "He has risen," and the other would respond "He has risen indeed." Even as Jesus rose to newness of life on Easter Sunday, so you can receive newness of spiritual life through the forgiveness of your sins. When Nicodemus came to Jesus and asked Him how he could live a godly life, Jesus said "You must be born again."[13] You can be born again when you accept Jesus Christ as your savior, and accept the gift He has given — forgiveness of your sins. How could we not accept such a gift?

Jesus also told His followers that He would come again at the end of time. During His first time on earth, Jesus came as a humble carpenter with no rank or prestige, and died a cruel death. When He returns, He will come as King of Kings and Lord of Lords. When He came the first time, a relatively small number of people recognized Him for who He was. At His second coming, the Bible says that everyone will see Him, and He will be recognized as the King of Kings in all His splendor and majesty. The Bible also says "That at the name of Jesus every knee should bow, in heaven and on earth and under the earth, and every tongue confess that Jesus Christ is Lord, to the glory of God the Father."[14] Our choice — yours and mine — is whether to bow our knees to Jesus Christ now, willingly, and receive forgiveness of sins and eternal life as God's children. Or, we can bow our knees in great regret at His coming, realizing that we've lost our opportunity to willingly welcome Him as our Savior and Lord. The choice is ours.

If you would like to accept Jesus Christ as your Savior today, you can go to the back of this book where it describes how you can ask Jesus Christ into your life. He came to earth to die for our sins and to be our Savior. Will you accept this gift of His love?

REASON 5

Changed Lives

John Newton was an English slave trader living in the 1700's. He was the captain of a slave ship that traveled from England to Africa to pick up hundreds of Africans and bring them back to England where they were sold as slaves. John was a tough sea captain in a cruel and demanding business, and he had no faith in God.

His life changed one day, when he accepted Jesus Christ as his personal Lord and Savior. John Newton experienced God's love and forgiveness and ended up leaving his job as captain of the slave ship. Years later, he wrote the song that begins like this: "Amazing grace, how sweet the sound, that saved a wretch like me. I once was lost, but now I'm found, was blind, but now, I see." We still sing that song — Amazing Grace — in churches today.

When Jesus came to earth, He spent much of His time not with the Pharisees, the religious leaders of the day, but with people whose lives needed changing. He was criticized for spending time with drunkards, tax gatherers, prostitutes and ordinary people. What was His response? "It is not the healthy who need a doctor, but the sick."[1] He said "The Son of Man came to seek and to save what was lost."[2]

This gives hope for you and for me. Do you have areas of your life that you wish you could change? Are there doubts or questions in your heart? Jesus came to seek and to save those who are lost. He has changed countless lives in history and He can touch your life as well.

In the first century, in the years following Christ's death and resurrection, there was a Jewish leader named Saul who zealously persecuted Christians, hauling them off to prison. One day when he was traveling to Damascus, Syria, Saul was knocked off his horse and saw a vision of Jesus Christ. Saul ended up committing his life to Christ and spreading the gospel throughout the world. Who was Saul? We know him now as the Apostle Paul, who wrote many of the books in the Bible. It was

Paul who wrote "If any one is in Christ, he is a new creation; the old has gone, the new has come!"[3]

Jesus Christ can make your life new. Some of us may be happy with many areas of our lives, but our spirits are dead to God. Not everyone who comes to Christ is an alcoholic or drug addict who needs major changes in their lives, but all of us need to be born again to God.

A Jewish leader named Nicodemus came to Jesus. Nicodemus was a respectable man, a leader in his community and probably well off materially. It was to Nicodemus that Jesus said "No one can see the kingdom of God unless he is born again."[4] The reason is that all of us — rich or poor, no matter how respectable we are — need a rebirth in our spirits, in our hearts and in our souls. Jesus also told Nicodemus "For God so loved the world that He gave His one and only Son, that whoever believes in Him shall not perish but have eternal life."[5] We don't have God in our hearts until we invite Him in by faith.

A man named Ben is a large land developer in California. One day he was taking a business acquaintance of his to see new homes in the Lake Tahoe area. The business acquaintance was a successful businessman who managed a business worth many millions of dollars. He was young and had many girlfriends. He appeared to have it all in this life. When they were done looking at the houses, the businessman asked Ben what Ben thought about getting married. He said he was thinking of settling down. This led to a conversation in which Ben talked about doing what is right before God. By the end of their conversation, the businessman had decided to ask Christ into his life. He knew that he had many issues to be sorted out in his life, but he did not let that stop him from committing his life to Jesus. As he got into his expensive sports car, he told Ben it had been the best day of his life.

God has the power to change lives. If you'd like to know how God can change lives, talk to some Christians whose lives have been changed. Ask them what changed in their lives when they asked Christ to be their savior. You may be surprised at the answers. For some people, the change may be subtle; they may notice more peace in their lives and have a real sense of God in their hearts. For others, the change may be dramatic.

For me personally, I was 20 years old when I became a Christian. I had been in college and was going through a time of trying to figure out what to do with the rest of my life. One day I met a Christian who introduced me to a community of people who had given their lives to Christ. Even though I did not have a Christian upbringing, I sensed that what they were saying was true, and three days later, I accepted Christ into my life.

How about you? No matter what is in your life, God has the power to give you a fresh start. The Bible says "To all who received Him, to those who believed in His name, He gave the right to become children of God."[6] The Apostle Paul said "If you confess with your mouth, 'Jesus is Lord,' and believe in your heart that God raised Him from the dead, you will be saved."[7]

One man who experienced this was Chuck Colson. He was the attorney for U.S. President Nixon at the time of the famous Watergate scandal in 1973. Chuck was known as Nixon's "hatchet man," and even boasted that he would walk over his own grandmother for the President. As a result of the Watergate scandal, Chuck was convicted and sent to prison — a huge downfall for someone who had been the lawyer to the President of the Unites States.

During the time of his trial, Chuck began meeting with Doug, a Christian minister, and Chuck eventually gave his life to Jesus Christ. He wrote the book of his life story and entitled it "Born Again." Chuck then went on to start a prison ministry as the result of his own experiences in prison.

A California businessman named Rob met his wife Terry after each of them had gone through a divorce. Terry was Jewish, and both she and Rob were studying new age philosophies. They met, fell in love and were married. Shortly after that, one of their spiritual advisors became a Christian and directed them to a Christian counselor. Soon Rob and Terry began to see that the new age philosophy they had been involved in could not provide lasting spiritual fulfillment and they gave their lives to Jesus Christ. Today, Rob and Terry are committed followers of Jesus Christ.

Each person's story is different, but they have a common theme — God can change lives. Look around you, and you may find others whose lives have been changed. Whatever your circumstances, wherever you are, God can change your life too if you will let Him.

REASON 6

How Long Is
Eternity?

To three year old Johnny traveling in a car to Disneyland, time seems to go by very slowly. He asks every ten minutes, "Mommy, how soon are we going to get there?" and the two hour car ride seems to him like an eternity. Once that three year old gets to Disneyland, however, hours can go by in a flash, and after eight hours, Johnny is asking "But mommy, we just got here, can't I stay some more?"

Einstein, in his famous theory of relativity, put forth the proposition that even time itself can be relative — it can vary when connected with the speed of light. Even though our minds may struggle to comprehend this, we all know the difference between looking at a clock, anxiously counting seconds waiting for something to end, and having an enjoyable experience where it seems like hours go by in seconds.

What about eternity? The Bible says that all of our life here on earth is like a fleeting shadow. "As for man, his days are like grass, he flourishes like a flower of the field; the wind blows over it and it is gone, and its place remembers it no more."[1]

You can stop to think for a second how brief life really is. As I write this, I am 53 years old. In some ways it seems like I've lived a long time and have had a lot of experiences. In other ways, life seems like it has been pretty short.

What about you? How do you think about time and eternity? The Bible says "Man is destined to die once, and after that to face judgement."[2] Most major world religions believe that human beings are more than just flesh and blood — they believe that we have a soul or spirit that lives on after our physical bodies die. Seen in the light of eternity, our lifespan can seem very short. A bumper sticker could put it like this: "Life is short and then you're dead a long time."

We were created for eternity. Our life on earth is very short and temporary. When we think that the pleasures of this earth are the entire meaning of life, we can be bitterly disappointed.

In light of eternity, how should we live our lives here on earth? What happens to us after we die? These are key questions that every thinking person ought to consider. Picture an ancient Indian tribe with its customs surrounding death. That tribe, instead of viewing death as the end, simply views it as the soul leaving the body. If the "real you" is your soul, and your body is just your temporary home, then we ought to pay much greater attention to our eternal home.

The Old Testament in the Bible begins with the words "In the beginning God." [3] The Book of John in the New Testament, referring to Jesus as the Word, starts with "In the beginning was the Word, and the Word was with God, and the Word was God…Through Him all things were made; without Him nothing was made that has been made." [4] God has existed for all eternity and will continue to exist for all eternity. He exists in a realm beyond time and space, but He also touches our lives here on this earth. The Bible says "The length of our days is seventy years — or eighty, if we have the strength…"[5] In the light of eternity, our life here on earth is like the twinkling of an eye.

What is eternity like? What happens after our soul leaves the temporary home of this body? A common theme of most major religions is that in the next life we will reap the consequences of our choices and actions here in this life. The Bible says "For the wages of sin is death, but the gift of God is eternal life in Christ Jesus our Lord." [6] The Bible teaches us that, after we die, there will be a day of judgment in which our soul will appear before God.

Many people who have had near death experiences, when they almost die then come back to life, report one of two types of experiences. Some people feel a great sense of peace and see a great light. A different group of people feel loneliness and darkness. This loneliness and darkness could be a foretaste of what the Bible calls "hell," which is also described in word pictures in the Bible. One word picture is of flames and torment; another refers to outer darkness. Although our human minds may not be able to comprehend this exactly, it seems clear that hell will include being separated forever from God as a just punishment for our sins.

Heaven is the place where you will eternally live with God if you have been forgiven through faith in Christ. The Bible describes heaven using various pictures, but it may be hard for us to exactly imagine what heaven is like. The Bible cautions us that "'No eye has seen, no ear has heard, no mind has conceived what God has prepared for those who love Him' — but God has revealed it to us by His Spirit."[7] One picture of heaven from the book of Revelation in the Bible is of a beautiful city with streets of gold. What we do know is that we will live in the presence of God. The Bible says that God will wipe away all tears and sorrow. There will be no need for the sun, because the glory of God will be our light. We will dwell in the presence of Jesus Christ forever.

How can we get to heaven? How can you live in a place filled with the holiness of God who is perfect and has never sinned? It seems clear that if everyone on earth simply went to heaven exactly as is, then heaven itself would no longer be heaven; it would be filled with our pride, our lust, our greed and our selfishness. The Bible outlines how we can get to heaven. God in His love and mercy sent His only Son, Jesus Christ, to die on the cross for our sins, so we could be forgiven. When you accept the gift of Jesus Christ, your sins are forgiven and your soul is wiped clean. It is a fresh start and you can enter heaven as a child of God.

Which way will you choose? You could hope that most major religions are wrong and that we really do not have a soul or spirit. You could hope that when you are dead, you are dead, and your soul really won't live on forever. Or, you can choose to accept the gift of God which is eternal life through Jesus Christ. The choice is yours. I invite you to read the section "The Four Spiritual Laws" at the end of this book to find out how you can accept the gift of eternal life in Jesus Christ.

The Four
Spiritual Laws

Just as there are physical laws that govern the physical universe, so are there spiritual laws that govern your relationship with God.

1. God **LOVES** you and offers a wonderful **PLAN** for your life.

(References contained in the Four Spiritual Laws are from the Bible and should be read in context wherever possible.)

God's Love
"God so loved the world that He gave His one and only Son, that whoever believes in Him shall not perish, but have eternal life" (John 3:16 NIV).

God's Plan

[Christ speaking] "I came that they might have life, and might have it abundantly" [that it might be full and meaningful] (John 10:10).

Why is it that most people are not experiencing the abundant life? Because...

2. Man is SINFUL and SEPARATED from God. Therefore, he cannot know and experience God's love and plan for his life.

Man Is Sinful

"All have sinned and fall short of the glory of God" (Romans 3:23). Man was created to have fellowship with God; but, because of his stubborn self-will, he chose to go his own independent way, and fellowship with God was broken. This self-will, characterized by an attitude of active rebellion or passive indifference, is an evidence of what the Bible calls sin.

Man Is Separated

"The wages of sin is death" [spiritual separation from God] (Romans 6:23).

This diagram illustrates that God is holy and man is sinful. A great gulf separates the two. The arrows illustrate that man is continually trying to reach God and the abundant life through his own efforts, such as a good life, philosophy, or religion — but he inevitably fails.

The third law explains the only way to bridge this gulf...

3. Jesus Christ is God's ONLY provision for man's sin. Through Him you can know and experience God's love and plan for your life.

He Died in Our Place

"God demonstrates His own love toward us, in that while we were yet sinners, Christ died for us" (Romans 5:8).

He Rose From the Dead

"Christ died for our sins...He was buried...He was raised on the third day, according to the Scriptures...He appeared to Peter, then to the twelve. After that He appeared to more than five hundred..." (1 Corinthians 15:3-6).

He Is the Only Way to God

"Jesus said to him, 'I am the way, and the truth, and the life; no one comes to the Father, but through Me'" (John 14:6).

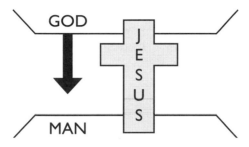

This diagram illustrates that God has bridged the gulf which separates us from Him by sending His Son, Jesus Christ, to die on the cross in our place to pay the penalty for our sins.

It is not enough just to know these three laws...

4. We must individually RECEIVE Jesus Christ as Savior and Lord; then we can know and experience God's love and plan for our lives.

We Must Receive Christ
"As many as received Him, to them He gave the right to become children of God, even to those who believe in His name" (John 1:12)

We Receive Christ Through Faith
"By grace you have been saved through faith; and that not of yourselves, it is the gift of God; not as a result of works, that no one should boast" (Ephesians 2:8,9).

When We Receive Christ, We Experience a New Birth
(Read John 3:1-8.)

We Receive Christ by Personal Invitation

[Christ speaking] "Behold, I stand at the door and knock; if any one hears My voice and opens the door, I will come in to him" (Revelation 3:20).

Receiving Christ involves turning to God from self (repentance) and trusting Christ to come into our lives to forgive our sins and to make us what He wants us to be. Just to agree intellectually that Jesus Christ is the Son of God and that He died on the cross for our sins is not enough. Nor is it enough to have an emotional experience. We receive Jesus Christ by faith, as an act of the will.

These two circles represent two kinds
of lives:

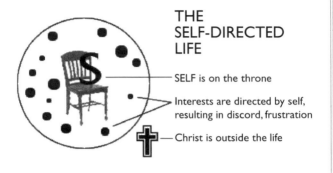

THE
SELF-DIRECTED
LIFE

— SELF is on the throne

— Interests are directed by self,
resulting in discord, frustration

— Christ is outside the life

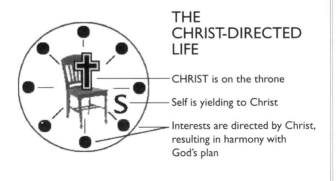

THE
CHRIST-DIRECTED
LIFE

— CHRIST is on the throne

— Self is yielding to Christ

— Interests are directed by Christ,
resulting in harmony with
God's plan

Which circle best describes your life?
Which circle would you like to have
represent your life?

*The following explains how you can receive
Christ:*

You can receive Christ right now by faith through prayer

(Prayer is talking to God)

God knows your heart and is not so
concerned with your words as He is with
the attitude of your heart. The following is a
suggested prayer:

*"Lord Jesus, I need You. Thank You for dying on
the cross for my sins. I open the door of my life
and receive You as my Savior and Lord. Thank
You for forgiving my sins and giving me eternal
life. Take control of the throne of my life. Make
me the kind of person You want me to be."*

Does this prayer express the desire of your heart? If it does, I invite you to pray this prayer right now and Christ will come into your life, as He promised.

I invite you to contact us at www.GodLovesTheWorld.com so we can answer any questions or send you information to help you grow as a Christian. May God bless you.

© Copyright 1965, 2000, 2004 Campus Crusade for Christ, Inc.

Scripture References

REASON 1 — THE WONDER OF NATURE
[1] Genesis 1:1
[2] Isaiah 45:18
[3] Psalm 19:1
[4] Job 36:26
[5] Genesis 1:27
[6] Romans 1:20
[7] Genesis 1:1

REASON 2 — WHAT ABOUT GOOD AND EVIL?
[1] Luke 6:31
[2] Mark 12:31
[3] Psalm 119:160
[4] 1 John 4:8
[5] Galatians 5:22
[6] Galatians 5:20
[7] Proverbs 16:25

REASON 3 — OUR EMPTY HEARTS
[1] Ecclesiastes 1:3
[2] Ecclesiastes 2:11
[3] Hebrews 13:5

[4] John 14:27
[5] Philippians 4:6, 7
[6] Psalms 16:11

REASON 4 — WHO IS JESUS?

[1] Matthew 2:4–6
[2] Mark 2:5
[3] Mark 2:7
[4] Mark 2:9–12
[5] John 11:25–27
[6] John 11:39, 40
[7] John 11:43
[8] John 6:35, 51
[9] Matthew 26:53
[10] Luke 23:34
[11] Luke 23:46
[12] Luke 24:5, 6
[13] John 3:7
[14] Philippians 2:10, 11

REASON 5 — CHANGED LIVES

[1] Mark 2:17
[2] Luke 19:10
[3] 2 Corinthians 5:17
[4] John 3:3

[5] John 3:16
[6] John 1:12
[7] Romans 10:9

Reason 6 — How Long is Eternity?
[1] Psalm 103:15
[2] Hebrews 9:27
[3] Genesis 1:1
[4] John 1:1, 3
[5] Psalm 90:10
[6] Romans 6:23
[7] 1 Corinthians 2:9, 10